How To Get More Prospects, Customers, Sales and Profits For Your Business Using 7 Proven Marketing Secrets

Mark Hendricks

SmallBizSuccessCoach.com

Legal Notices: Neither the Author or the Publisher assumes any responsibility for errors, inaccuracies or omissions. Any slights of people or organizations are unintentional. If advice concerning tax, legal or related matters is needed, the services of a qualified professional should be sought. This book is not intended for use as a source of legal, accounting or financial advice. Also some suggestions made in this book concerning sales and marketing and business practices may have inadvertently introduced practices deemed unlawful in certain states or municipalities. You should be aware of the various laws governing advertising, sales, marketing and other business practices in your particular industry and in your marketplace.

The Publisher also notes that certain offers of books, tapes, other products and services have been made in this book and reserves the right to modify or withdraw those offers at any time.

DEDICATION

To all entrepreneurs who dare to
dream big, you are the heroes.

CONTENTS

READ THIS FIRST!

If you're looking to grow your business profits, then you'll find this book very valuable in helping you make more money, without working harder, and in less time than you're spending now.

In it, you'll discover how to grow your business profits by:

- attracting more leads and prospects to your business
- converting more prospects to customers for your business, and
- increasing the lifetime profit value of your current and new customers by increasing the average dollars per sale, and increasing the frequency that they purchase from you

Plus, you'll learn these seven important marketing secrets that most business owners never systematically program into their business for consistent results:

1. How to clearly state the exact 'reasons why' people should do business with you rather than any of your competitors
2. How to improve your current marketing approach for quick profits
3. Three secrets to getting more profits out of your current customers
4. How to set up joint venture alliances with other business owners – a mutually beneficial way to easily harvest more profits by working together with others
5. How to use targeted direct marketing to get new customers who are eager and willing to do business with you
6. How to get more results from your advertising dollars – your advertising is costing you the same whether it brings in a little or a lot, here's how to get more business in the door with no more expense
7. How to drive your competition absolutely crazy by using FREE marketing concepts – don't pay for advertising, when you can get it for FREE

Okay, let's get started…

Hi, my name is Mark Hendricks.

I'm a marketing expert and business success coach who gets you more prospects, customers, sales, and profits – and most importantly, the real benefit of all that… the lifestyle that a successful business can give you and yours!

Now I know you're thinking, "So why is this guy telling me all this, why should I believe anything he says, and why should I care?" – good questions, here's why…

You see, most business owners I come across don't have the time or expertise in marketing to really leverage all the upside profit potential that lies hidden in their business. In plain talk, they're already 'wearing too many hats' and just too busy working **in** their business rather than **on** their business, to make it as profitable as it could and should be.

And that's what this book is all about.

You're going to learn seven marketing concepts, ideas, and strategies that can be implemented into your business that will literally bring you thousands, or tens of thousands, or hundreds of thousands of extra dollars for little or no risk, no effort, and no increased expense.

All of these ideas will help you generate more profits from your business by leveraging assets or advertisements or customers or opportunities that you most likely already have in place, but have never had the time or knowledge to leverage to their full profit potential. You'll learn why it works, and prove it to yourself as well.

Enough talk, let's get going with the…

"Three Ways To Grow Your Business"
(actually, I will tell you five)

First, let's talk about a deceptively simple concept that once you grasp its full potential, everything else in this book will become crystal clear and very valuable to you.

Unfortunately, it's at this very first concept that some business people dismiss this as 'obvious', and don't fully grasp this foundational truth of business building, therefore they completely miss out on how this simple concept will catapult your profits beyond what you are currently doing, and help turn your business into the profit-machine it can and will be.

Okay, having said that...

Let's say you want to increase your profits by 50% this year.

Now let's take a look at the numbers (let's use $100,000 for easy math)...

$100,000 + 50% growth = $150,000

Yes, I know that's a simple formula, and I know you're thinking..."Mark, I've been busting my brain for years trying to make my business have more profits – if it were that easy, I'd just wave a *magic wand* and do it."

Let me introduce you to the magical concept of the *"Magic Wand of Marketing Leverage"* in helping you build your business.

First, let's talk about "The Three Ways To Grow Your Business":

- **attracting more prospects**
- **converting more prospects to customers**
- **increasing the lifetime value of your current and new customers by increasing the average dollars per sale, and increasing the frequency that they purchase from you**

> **** Important – please read through these three ways to grow your business again ****

Alright, let's continue...

So, instead of hoping for 'pie-in-the-sky' dreams of increasing your business by 50%, we can break things down into manageable steps, and if we increase each of these three areas just a little, we create the magical effect of **"Marketing Leverage"**, like this...

$100,000...

- *plus* **15% increase in attracting more prospects**
- *plus* **15% increase in converting more prospects to customers**
- *plus* **15% increase in sales from current and new customers**

Simply by increasing <u>each</u> of these three areas by only 15%, your profits grow *exponentially* to...

$152,087 !!

So you can appreciate how important it is to have a marketing program in place that leverages <u>each </u>of these three basic areas.

Now here's a little secret that can work **_more_** magic for you...

In each of these three areas you've seen work above, there are a number of strategies and techniques that can be used to leverage up each of these three basic areas even **_more_**, creating more marketing leverage to increase the profits of your company.

So instead of only 15% leverage in each of these, it's not unreasonable to think we could leverage one (or more) of these three marketing levers up to 50% or more!

Stop, and just imagine for a moment...what if you could:

- **attract 50% more prospects, or...**
- **convert 50% more prospects to customers, or...**
- **increase the lifetime value of your current and new customers by increasing the average dollars per sale by 50%, and/or increase the frequency that they purchase from you by 50%**

What would that do to the bottom line profits of your business?

Gets exciting, doesn't it?

So, you can really see the advantages of **"Marketing Leverage"** and how this one concept can create astounding results in your business, yes?

You're with me so far, right?

Good.

Remember, I promised you on the first page that I'd reveal all my secrets of how you can build your business profits. This one simple concept (even if you read no further) will have a tremendous effect on your profits.

And for many business owners, this one singular concept opens your eyes to a whole new way of looking at your business, wouldn't you agree?

And here's a bonus tip…

Here's a fourth and a fifth way to leverage your profits:

- increase the rate at which those first three happen... equals more profits in less time!
- increase your sales profit margins by reducing your cost of goods sold

Before reading on, I'd suggest you read this section one more time, and prove to yourself how this one concept can have a *dramatic effect* on your thinking and your results.

Okay, let's move on to the seven proven marketing strategies, the first of which is your 'good ol' USA'...

Secret One...

"What's Your USA?"

The first thing to do is define just what it is that differentiates you from your competitors in a very beneficial way to your prospects and customers.

You want to identify the unique benefit, appeal, or big promise that you offer the customer that no one else offers.

This is what will be the core of your marketing plan – everything else we do will be dependent on identifying your USA (or USA's for different market segments).

I find most businesses can't clearly articulate what makes their business, or products and services unique to their marketplace.

It's just not good enough to say "We have the best quality products, price, and service", everybody says that, therefore it doesn't make you unique, does it?

And no, I'm not talking about a 'slogan', like so many that you hear or see from the 'big' companies, dreamed up by highly-paid ad agencies, that state no benefit to the customers. (although there have been good 'slogans' that were really great USAs (such as, "Hot, fresh pizza in 30 minutes...or it's free." – remember that one?)

So, exactly what is your USA?

By USA, I mean your...

Unique Selling Advantage

You need to be able to tell your customers, in a very specific way, the 'reasons why' they should favor your business.

In formulating your USA, you answer the following questions:

- Why <u>should</u> customers do business with you rather than anyone else, or do what they're doing now, or do it themselves, or do nothing at all?
- Why <u>do</u> customers do business with you rather than anyone else, or do what they're doing now, or do it themselves, or do nothing at all?

By the way, these are not necessarily easy questions for you to answer.

It's because you, personally, are wrapped up in your business, and you *intuitively* understand your relationship with your customers, but most likely you've never attempted to clearly articulate your uniqueness, so it can be immediately evident to your prospects, customers, employees, and suppliers (in other words, all the people you have contact with) – the reasons why they do and should do business with you.

By developing clear answers to the questions above, you'll be ahead of 96% of all businesses who have never taken the time and effort to do so.

Here are a few ideas for good USAs...

- you sell your product/service for less
- you sell a higher quality product/service than others, and you charge more
- you provide more customer education or service, prior to and after the sale
- you offer a longer or better guarantee or warranty than your competition
- you offer more free bonuses, gifts, and services than others
- you offer a broader in-stock selection and choices

- you serve a specific niche market (age group, industry, or type of person)
- you offer quicker service than your competitors

For instance, in my marketing consulting work, my USA is...

"I get you more prospects, customers, sales and profits by turning your existing overlooked assets and hidden opportunities into new-found profits, and turn those profits into steady, on-going streams of income for you."

So the first secret to developing your **"Magic Wand of Marketing Leverage"** is to discover exactly what it is about your company that makes you unique and beneficial to your prospects and customers.

And use your USA in your ads, in your conversations with your customers and prospects, on your stationery, your business cards, your billing, your receipts, your website and blog, your emails – and make sure your salespeople and employees know, understand, and are able to communicate it to everyone they come in contact with too.

By discovering an effective USA, you'll attract more prospects, convert more prospects to customers, and get more profit from each customer on the initial sale, and get more ongoing revenue over the lifetime of your customer.

Okay, once we've got your USA, now we're ready to work on how we can leverage your current marketing for more profits...

Secret Two...

"Leveraging Your Current Marketing For More Profits"

The next step we work on is looking at what marketing strategies you're currently using, analyze their effectiveness, and use strategies and techniques to leverage what you're already doing to give you more 'bang for your marketing buck', at no extra cost.

It's amazing how much more money can be harvested by implementing some very simple, yet highly effective marketing strategies that cost you nothing, or little, to put into place – yet these strategies can yield double, triple or more the resulting profit just by making small incremental changes in what you're already doing.

Here's a few areas to explore:

- take a look at your current advertising and promotions, and test the various variables that can make your ads and promotions yield double, triple or more the results – for the same amount of money you're spending already (you've got the same fixed cost, why not leverage for maximum results?)
- how about your current sales training – could we implement successful strategies gleaned from your top salespeople, and train all your salespeople and employees to use these proven and profitable techniques?
- look at your conversion ratio of prospect-to-customer, and develop and implement strategies and techniques to improve these results for more first-time sales
- set up a plan for capturing all customer information to be used in followup contact with prospects and customers, and for future offers (this is very important)
- design strategies, offers, and packaged sales promotions to re-sell, up-sell, cross-sell, and back-end sell your customers to add more lifetime customer profitability to your business

In each of these areas above, we apply the USA that we've come up with in Secret One. We hammer home the USA in every way possible to show your prospects and customers, in every communication, what makes your business unique and give them the reasons why they should purchase from you because of the benefits you offer, and they receive by favoring your business above all others.

By developing these first two secrets – your USA, and analyzing and improving upon your current marketing, you'll see a vast improvement in your profits from the results of attracting more prospects, converting more prospects to customers, and getting more profit from each customer on the initial sale, plus the ongoing revenue that each customer provides you over the lifetime of your relationship with them.

Now let's move on and discover how to get the most out of your current customers...

Secret Three...

"Getting The Most Out Of Your Current Customers"

Okay, now we've got you an effective USA, and started to leverage the marketing you currently have in place, and have designed a system to capture customer and prospect information to keep in touch with them for future offers.

Wow, we've accomplished a lot already, haven't we?

Now...think back a few years...and remember when you first started your business...how did you get your first customers, how much time and money did you invest in attracting those customers to buy from you for the first time?

Most business owners forget just how hard (and expensive) it was to get your first customers.

Here's something that's very important for you to understand...

Did you know that's it's 20 times easier to sell existing customers than it is to sell to new prospects?

Why?

Because your customers already know you, like you, and trust you – and they like what your product/service has done for them.

You see, there's an interesting process that takes place in the mind of your prospects and customers before they will do business with you, or continue to do business with you.

They must...

- **#1 – <u>Know You</u>** – through personal selling, advertising or word-of-mouth
- **#2 – <u>Like You</u>** – people are very emotional creatures, people do business with people they like – they first decide emotionally (on a 'gut level') to do business with you, then they justify their buying decisions with logic
- **#3 – <u>Trust You</u>** – they must feel that you have their best interest at heart, and that you always are looking for ways to bring more value to them than they pay you for – by helping them solve their problems and provide solutions in helping them save time, save frustration, save money, make money, or be entertained – or hopefully, a combination of these things

Always remember, the greatest asset of your business is your customers.

Your accountant probably doesn't put a category called 'Customers' on your balance sheet of assets, but as your marketing and business success coach, I sure do.

These original customers cost you a lot in time, energy, and money to get them to know you, like you, and trust you enough to do business with you in the first place – and they're now your happy customers.

This is your greatest sales lead list you could ever have. It's your HOT list !!

Now you're ready to make all of your past work pay off...BIG-TIME!...year after year after year.

The three magic words that will build your business profits for years to come are...

"Back End Sales!"

And it's one of the most jealously-guarded secrets of any successful marketer.

It's actually such a simple concept.

You see, once your customer buys from you, it's light-years easier to get them to buy from you again. And it's so much cheaper, because you don't have to spend so much time and money to develop the original attraction, interest, desire, likeability, and trust to get them to take action to buy from you, like you did the first time.

There's basically three ways to work your back-end sales.

#1 – Re-selling

Re-selling is simply selling them the same thing they bought before.

For example, consumable products (like health and beauty products, car performance additives, etc., basically anything that is consumed and needed again on a regular basis), or reoccurring services (such as accounting or bookkeeping, writing services, consulting, internet services, etc.).

When looking for some product/service to market, always try to think of products/services that are 'consumables' that need to be purchased and used (or enjoyed) over and over and over again by your customer.

That in itself will give you tremendous back-end sales and profits.

#2 – Up-selling

Up-selling is getting your customers to buy a better, more expensive, or more up-scale products or services from you, or an additional item(s) at the time of their main purchase while they're in the buying mood.

Maybe it's a new service that will save them time or money, or a new product that does whatever they need to do faster and more efficient – or maybe it's just the upscale model of what they already bought and it has a few more 'bells and whistles' (advantages and benefits) that they would really enjoy now that they have had the introductory product or service.

It's really such an easy concept, but you've got to take the time and effort to put this strategy into your marketing program, and get your staff and sales people using this in every situation to harvest your rewards.

#3 – Cross-Selling

Cross-selling is getting your customers to buy something else that's related to the original product/service they purchased from you.

Let's see just how this could work for you...

I'm sure in your business there are ancillary products or services that can be packaged and offered that would provide solutions to your customers...in other words, accessories or add-ons they want or need to better their lives, or the enjoyment of their main purchase.

And I'm going to give you a little 'preview' of our next section right now, these products or services don't necessarily have to be things that you sell, you could 'joint venture' with other business owners (non-competitors, of course) who've already got quality products/services that you could recommend to your loyal customers (more about how this benefits everyone in the next section – and did you know, you'll be able to make money by letting your customers know about another business' offers? And create more goodwill with your customers too?

Does this discussion of getting more from your current customers give you any ideas?

Think about it for a minute…

- What are some things you can market to your customers as your back-end now?
- What could you be selling to your customers that you aren't now?
- Whose products/services could you use as back-end sales for you in a 'joint venture' relationship?
- Who could use your products/services as back-end sales in a 'joint venture' relationship with you?
- You could even market the products/services of other business owners who don't know that this can be done!

Okay, I digressed a little...so let's get back on track.

You've got to begin to understand that the first sale you make with your customer is just the beginning of a long lifetime relationship.

Always be asking yourself, "How do you bring more value, more products, more services to your customers during their buying lifetime with you?"

Basically, it comes down to this one question…

How to you become more valuable to your customers?

So how do you get the most out of your current customers?

Here's a few things we can do:

- create customer classifications using a computer database that will allow you to define precisely everything you can find about your customer, and what they like to buy, and how often
- come up with re-selling, up-selling, and cross-selling opportunities within your business that your customers have yet to purchase from you
- develop back-end products or services, especially packaging or bundling these together to add more perceived value to your customers in these continuing service and product purchases, and have them sign up for automatic service or product shipping, and pay you on an automatic payment plan
- consider the benefits of 'joint venture alliances' (see next section) with other businesses to leverage your customer base and back-end profits, and theirs too!

Just remember, your major investment into your business is always your front-end marketing to get your first sale with your customer.

After that, it's 20 times easier to make your sales through reselling, upselling, cross-selling and joint venturing with others.

By developing your USA, improving upon your current marketing, and getting more profits out of your current customers by using these techniques, you're now ready to learn how to leverage your business by creating joint venture marketing alliances with other business owners you already know, like and trust. Let's learn about this exciting concept now...

Secret Four...

"Joint Venture Marketing Alliances"

As you've learned already, you can get some fantastic profit results just leveraging the hidden assets I've been able to find in your business so far. In this section, you'll be in for a treat and be amazed at how creating joint venture marketing alliances will quickly and easily build your customer base, and build your business profits for years to come.

The Joint Venture Marketing Alliance concept is very simple, yet extremely powerful.

Remember how, in the last section, we discussed how long and hard and expensive it was for your business to get its first customers to know you, like you, and trust you?

Well, now we're going to have your business acquire new customers by using the 'hidden assets' (customers) of other businesses who have spent years and years, and tens or hundreds of thousand, or millions of dollars to develop their relationships with their customers who know, like, and trust them.

And you won't have to spend anywhere near the time or money they did in acquiring the customer the first time around.

You like this, don't you?

It's one of the most powerful marketing secrets I use – and you're now in the position to build your business off the trust that other business owners have already built with their customers over the years, and it's a win-win-win for everybody involved. For you, the other business, and their customers. In other words, it will be advantageous for other businesses to help you do this.

Why would other businesses be willing to do these joint venture alliances with you?

Here are the two major benefits to your joint venture ally:

- #1 – it's in their best interest to be of greater value and service to their customers, to help them find bargains and deals on quality services and products, just like I've shown you how to do in previous sections
- #2 – they will receive some form of compensation from you that they will benefit from, whether it be financial (a portion of the initial sale), or a service or product that you could provide them for themselves or their business

What's in it for you?

- #1 – it saves you time in acquiring new customers
- #2 – it saves you effort in acquiring new customers
- #3 – it saves you money in acquiring new customers

Just remember how much it really costs you in time, money and effort to acquire a new customer.

By using joint venture alliances (and you can do more than one at a time!), you'll be able to acquire new customers without the huge expense of prospecting, educating, and selling your prospects to become your customers – by using joint venture marketing alliances, you'll only be introduced to people who are ready to buy right now – this saves you tons of time, effort, and money!

The first place I suggest we look for joint venture alliance possibilities is your own customer list. By that I mean, you may have some business owners as your own customers who know, like, and trust you – who just need to be enlightened to how this joint venture concept can benefit them and their customers, and can work to their advantage.

Secondly, think about what other successful businesses your customers already do business with that have the same kind of customers that you have and want more of (note that these businesses are not necessarily in the same industry as yourself).

Setting up these alliances can take a variety of formats:

- letters or emails of endorsement to their customer list (a special offer only for their customers to introduce them to your business)
- cross promotions (you see kind of thing at all the time with major corporations, just think of the promotions you see with movies and the major fast-food chains – there's no reason you couldn't do the same with businesses in your market area, whether local, regional, or national)
- enclosing your promotional flyer in their communications, or in their 'new customer welcome kit' when someone buys from them the first time, whether this is digitally delivered or in print
- and other creative ways that have been successfully used

Of course, we'll need to set up systems to capture where your new customers are coming from (this is not hard to do using the internet and point of purchase systems that are implemented), so your joint venture ally can get the credit that is due.

Here's an interesting and profitable twist...

You can also structure these joint venture alliances using your list of customers, where you benefit from the goodwill and value you bring to your customers. This brings you easy profits by leveraging your relationship with your customers, and introducing them to other reputable businesses – who just need to be enlightened to how this joint venture concept can benefit them in acquiring new customers in the same manner I've revealed to you.

This is a very powerful and profitable concept that can be set up in a variety of ways to help you generate new customers and quick cash-flow, all without the high cost in time, effort, and money – and remember, all these new customers have the potential to bring you lifetime customer back-end profits for years to come.

We've developed your USA, improved your current marketing, your getting more profits out of your current customers, created joint marketing alliances, now let's learn a little about how you can use targeted direct marketing to get new customers...

Secret Five...

"Targeted Direct Response Marketing To Get New Customers"

Have you ever stopped to think about what business you're in?

Seems like a silly question, doesn't it?

When most business owners or executives answer this question, they usually say, "We're in the such-and-such business. We make/sell/provide widgets." (or some type of service).

Actually, I'd like you to begin thinking with a little different 'mindset'.

From this moment on, **you're actually in the business of _marketing_ your business**, that happens to be in the such-and-such business, and that makes/sells/provides widgets (or some type of service).

This one little twist has had a tremendous effect on many successful business owners.

You must realize that you first must be a marketer (or have an effective marketing coach working with you) to drive more business to your door, implement procedures to serve your customers, and create a profitable on-going enterprise.

With that said, let's talk about using Targeted Direct Response Marketing To Get New Customers.

First, what do I mean by...

Targeted Direct Response Marketing

Too many businesses run ads, send emails, run commercials, create websites, or mail flyers, etc. – that do no more than list their company's name and address, and maybe their phone number.

Just look through the newspaper, or on the internet, or TV commercials, or radio spots, or business cards – it's just the 'name, rank, and serial number' approach to 'getting your name out there'.

This is absolutely the worst form of advertising you could possible do.

It does nothing to benefit your prospect or customer at all, and is a complete waste of your money.

By the way, don't you just love it when the media rep or your ad agency tells you that "you've got to just keep getting your name out there"?

They're not paying for the ad bills, are they?

Actually, they're making money – while your ads are just 'getting your name out there', without bringing you customers and profits – *this is not good!*

Promise, promise, promise – that you'll <u>never</u> ever again, do any marketing that:

- does not make a specific offer to your prospect or customer
- does not ask them to respond (in one way or another)
- does not tell them how to respond to get what you're offering, and respond right now!

You should always think of your advertising as thousands of salesmen working for you.

Think of it as 'Salesmanship in print', if you wish. If one of your salesmen didn't produce sales for you, you wouldn't keep him very long, would you?

Well, if your ad, email, website, postcard, telemarketing, or flyer doesn't pull sales immediately upon running it (or at least generates leads, if that's its intent), then something needs to change – and fast!

As you may know, there are six distinctive parts of a highly profitable ad – one of which has the proven power to produce 17 times the results over other approaches.

Just think, the ad or promotion you're paying the same dollar amount for each time you run it could be producing double, triple or more the response than it is now. Using this one **"Magic Wand of Marketing Leverage"** could bring in more business than you could know what to do with!

Here's the six-step process of Targeted Direct Response Marketing:

- make sure you've got your USA fine-tuned toward the target markets you serve best
- look closely at your customer base (basically you want more of these types of people)
- research how you can best get your offer in the hands of, or seen by, or heard by, your target market (whether it be mailing lists for direct mail and phone calls, trade shows, internet, emails, faxes, flyers, door-hangers, newspapers, magazines, TV, radio, etc.)

- consider which of these methods is most cost effective in reaching your target market
- test your targeted list (just a small sample test first), test your offers, test your pricing, and other variables to find which promotion is most successful in producing the best results for the dollar cost invested
- then roll out your tested and proven promotion in a big way to all your targeted market and enjoy all the extra profits that you've been missing out on

These steps can be used in attracting new customers, converting old prospects to new customers, and back-end selling your current customers too.

Target Direct Response Marketing can work for any business if structured properly.

It's just that most businesses have been led to believe that 'getting your name out there' is good enough reason for someone to call you, or pay a visit to your store, or place an order with you. This type of so-called 'institutional' or 'image' marketing doesn't pay its way, and you should <u>not</u> be using it.

For your marketing to work (in other words, <u>make you money right now</u>), it's got to be Targeted Direct Response Marketing, which is designed to stimulate an immediate response from your targeted prospect, and get them to become a customer in the shortest period of time, and at the least amount of cost to you. Then you've got something that will work for a long, long time in getting you more profits for your business.

Okay, let's review again...we've developed your USA, improved your current marketing, your getting more profits out of your current customers, created joint marketing alliances, learned more about how you can use targeted direct marketing to get new customers, how about learning how to get more results from your advertising dollars...

Secret Six...

"Getting More Response From Your Advertising Dollars"

In the last section, I brought up the point that your advertising costs are the same, whether your ad makes zero dollars, modest dollars, or many dollars for you.

You are paying for ad space, or airtime, or internet services, or printing and postage costs of flyers, postcards, letters, plus the creative talent work that goes into developing the promotion.

And these are your fixed costs.

I'm going to reveal to you one of the greatest marketing secrets ever discovered.

It's these three simple little words...

Test – Test – Test

I am astonished how most business owners don't make calculated small tests to see what effect different headlines, stories, propositions, offers, guarantees, time deadlines, payment plans, and calls to action have on the response they get to their marketing and advertising efforts.

I already mentioned (in the last section) that one of things I just listed in the previous paragraph has been proven to increase the response of an ad or promotion by 17 times (do you know which one?) – just think how that would affect the profitability of your business!

Even if you could produce double, triple or greater the response, you'd have gained tremendous leverage in your business, both on the front-end sales and your back-end profits too, wouldn't you?

You see, that's how powerful this marketing stuff really is.

It's your *last* advantage to exploit – it's where you can differentiate you and your business from all your competitors, and make your business wildly profitable, and make large deposits to your bank account.

Beware, your accountant and banker may start asking how you're making all this money!

You can tell them you found a **"Magic Wand"**.

So, what can we do to make your ads, and other promotions pull better?

Let's begin looking at each part of your ad or promotion, and testing each one, one at a time to see if we can get more response (kind of like the 'scientific method' we learned in junior high).

Here's the method in a nutshell:

- come up with an ad or offer and run it
- measure the results
- think about <u>one</u> thing we could change to make it better
- run the ad again with the <u>one</u> change
- measure the results
- continue this process until the <u>one</u> thing we've changed produces measurably greater results

Then, guess what – we change <u>one</u> of the <u>other</u> six basic parts of the ad, measure the results, think how to make that one thing better, measure the results, and continue the process until that one part of your ad is producing measurably greater results – and so on, until you've tweaked every part of the ad and have leveraged up your results by 2x, 3x 5x, 10x's or more!

But we don't stop there – we'll keep asking 'how high is high?' – and come up with other approaches or use different media, or other ways to get your message to your market.

This secret, and the other five we've already discussed, is how I use my "**Magic Wand of Marketing Leverage**" to generate more profits in any business, yours included.

Okay, one secret to go – we've developed your USA, improved your current marketing, your getting more profits out of your current customers, created joint marketing alliances, learned more about how you can use targeted direct marketing to get new customers, found how to get more results from your advertising dollars, now let's drive your competition absolutely crazy by using FREE marketing concepts...

Secret Seven...

"Using FREE Marketing That Drives Your Competition Crazy"

Don't you just love that word...FREE?

So does everyone else.

As a matter of fact, in a study of the most powerful marketing words, FREE is at the top of the list.

So how can you get your message to your market for FREE?

Before I tell you, I want to make sure you remember just how much it used to cost you in time, effort and money to get a new customer – what I'm about to reveal to you is a way for you to get your marketing message delivered FREE to your market. And if you want to get a great response with this, then you're going to have to come up with a great 'reason why' people should immediately respond in droves, once they receive your offer.

Here's what we do...

Come up with an irresistible introductory special offer deal for new customers (or current customers too) that could be freely distributed by:

- other businesses as a special bonus to their prospects and customers
- businesses to their employees
- clubs and organizations to their members
- schools to their staff, students and parents
- non-profit groups to their supporters
- your customers as a gift to their friends

- you to your customers
- the media as a special deal for their customers
- and any others we can think of

All the marketing 'magnets' above are always looking for ways to benefit and do something nice for their people, and your special irresistible offer could be one of the best benefits they've ever promoted to their people.

Given half a minute, I bet we can think of 3 to 5 (minimum) in each of these categories that would do this in a second...if we come up with the right special offer for their circles of influence.

Basically, by using this simple concept, you've gotten your message to your market by way of a FREE delivery system. We create the email, or the master sheet flyers, or coupons, or a little 'present this for a 10% discount' card, or whatever – and they can reproduce as many as they want, and give away as many as they want.

Of course, you'll want to control the deadline to your offer (for a few reasons), and you may want to limit quantities, etc. – but you must be as generous as you possibly can be with your special deal offer.

What you are doing is...

Creating 'Word-Of-Mouth' Advertising
Out Of Thin Air...

... and you're being given an implied endorsement for FREE by the group that is 'giving away' your special deal as a perk to their group.

When you do this, we'll want to make your offer as irresistible as you possibly can so everyone will see what a great deal they're getting (and giving), by YOU helping them out.

Please understand that your message will be quickly distributed to hundreds, or thousands, or millions of prospects!

Now you and I both realize how you benefit when a bunch of new customers come your way, don't we? – you've gotten new prospects and customers for FREE, you get their customer info in your database and begin your lifetime relationship and back-end profits with them...

"This marketing leverage stuff is simply amazing!"

Here's some other ways to get FREE exposure for your business:

- send out press releases to the media or PR sites on the internet on newsworthy topics in your industry
- give tours of your business to clubs, organizations, schools, etc.
- make speeches to civic, business, or community organizations
- sponsor seminars, workshops or demonstrations related to your products or services (either you speaking, or bring in an outside special guest speaker)
- make charitable contributions that give you positive public exposure (I'm not talking about just giving money here – you need to get something tangible in return, like the promotion idea above. Or use the free distribution idea above as a fundraiser for non-profit groups – for each coupon redeemed, they get a portion of the sale – they raise money, you get good 'word-of-mouth', and you get new customers to build your back-end profits for years to come – another win-win-win situation!)

You can do these things yourself, or delegate some or all of these things these things to others who are capable to represent your interests. All these techniques will help position you and your business in a very favorable light

With all the strategies I've listed here in this section, remember that you are only paying for <u>results</u> (not ad space, or air time. etc.) – *just <u>results</u>* – which is exactly what I've promised you from the very beginning of this book, isn't it?

Let's sum this up...

We've developed your USA, improved your current marketing, your getting more profits out of your current customers, created joint marketing alliances, learned more about how you can use targeted direct marketing to get new customers, found how to get more results from your advertising dollars, and you learned how I can drive your competition absolutely crazy by using FREE marketing concepts.

Now that I've revealed to you everything in detail I promised I would, I'd like you to consider what I'm offering you. As you'll understand, it's an offer that will benefit you greatly....

"How To Make Lots More Money From The Ideas I've Given You In This Book"

My new friend, we've come a long way together in this short book, and you know at this point I specialize in coaching business owners on how to implement results-oriented marketing strategies and concepts that leverage the profitability of your business.

Let me explain how my approach is very different from others who hang out their shingle as a 'marketing guru' or 'consultant' to business owners.

Others…

- spend very little time getting to personally know you and your business
- spend little effort in educating you in the basic marketing principles and strategies that you need to know
- sell you their sales system or marketing package
- get your money and give you *some* support, and then…
- leave it up to you to try and make it work for yourself.

"As you may have guessed – I work very differently with my clients."

Here's what you get from my on-going personal guidance, experience and assistance…

- *How to attract more leads and prospects to your business*
- **How to convert more prospects to customers for your business**
- *How to increase the lifetime profit value of your current and new customers by increasing the average dollars per sale, and increasing the frequency that they purchase from you*
- **How to clearly state the exact *'reasons why'* people should do business with you rather than any of your competitors**
- *How to improve your current marketing approach for quick profits*
- **Three secrets to getting more profits out of your current customers**
- *How to set up joint venture alliances with other business owners – a mutually beneficial way to easily harvest more profits by working together with others*
- **How to use targeted direct marketing to get new customers who are eager and willing to do business with you**
- *How to get more results from your advertising dollars – your advertising is costing you the same whether it brings in a little or a lot, here's how to get more business in the door with no more expense*

- **How to drive your competition absolutely crazy by using FREE marketing concepts – don't pay for advertising, when you can get it for FREE**

Now even though I've presented these concepts in a very logical sequence, if you're like most business owners, in addition to all the other responsibilities (and headaches) you have in running your business…

- you don't really have the time or desire to figure out all of this stuff by yourself
- you won't follow through and put these strategies in place like you know you should, and…
- you know in your heart-of-hearts you're not capturing all the profit your business has to offer, and you could really use some expert help at this stage of your game

You'd agree, wouldn't you?

I've probably given you more in this one book than you know what to do with, or even begin to know what to do with!

That's where I can help you the most.

I've developed a variety of ways I can help you grow your business, it really depends on the best way to 'plug me in' to your company at this point in its growth.

You can see, I'm a specialist at doing something for busy business owners like yourself, that no one else you know can do for you…

"I get you more prospects, customers, sales and profits by turning your existing overlooked assets and hidden opportunities into new-found profits, and turn those profits into steady, on-going streams of income for you."

It's not at all unrealistic to think that I could bring you thousands, or tens of thousands, or hundreds of thousands of extra dollars (or more) for no risk, no effort, and no investment whatsoever on your part – depending on the level of service you're ready for.

Here's my problem (and I think a very attractive solution that you'll be interested in)…

I can only take on a few one-on-one personal marketing and success coaching clients at a time, but I also know there are thousands of business owners who could really use some help in attracting prospects, converting them to customers and clients, and then developing those buyers into long-term profitable relationships.

This is why I created the website and membership program called…

SmallBizSuccessCoach.com

By setting up this website I'm able to help more business owners learn and implement these proven strategies, and also help them understand and acquire the mindset it takes to be a successful entrepreneur.

Let me be clear, I'm not trying to sell you a pre-packaged marketing system. No, I prefer to teach you my jealously-guarded marketing and business secrets that I've discovered, tested and implemented into my own businesses and other businesses to generates millions upon millions of dollars of sales over the years.

By doing this, I can implant these marketing and success strategies into your mindset, so you have the power to create more and more successful results, time and time again.

Through audios, videos, special reports and study guides, webinars, teleconferences, articles, interviews and personal one-on-one call-in consultation days, workshops, bootcamps, and conferences too – you'll soon find that I've become your most trusted mentor, coach, and biggest fan too.

(I love creating "eagles", it's a purpose of mine – ask me sometime what I mean by that…there's an interesting story there)

Through the SmallBizSuccessCoach.com membership program, you receive my continuous guidance, support and teamwork to help you make more money in less time, which gives you what you really want… which is more lifestyle!

What's the catch?

There is no catch.

It's as simple at that.

With this results-oriented philosophy I have – believe me when I tell you, I'm very motivated to get you very successful and profitable results.

"In just a few months, you could increase your profits by 50% or more!"

If what I've said makes sense to you and catches your interest, simply go to the website and click around. There you'll find complete details of everything that the Small Biz Success Coach program includes (you can access those details by clicking the navigation link at the top that references the SBSC program)… that's SmallBizSuccessCoach.com

After looking and listening to all the information on the website, if you still have a question or two and just need a little personal contact with me before joining, pick up your phone and give me a call, 24 hours, at **352-583-3697** (it rings on my desk).

If I'm available I will pickup (so don't be surprised if you hear my voice).

If I'm not available, then please leave a message to let me know a few times you would be available to talk. I'll get back with you to answer your questions and give you an honest idea if this SBSC program is right for you.

Interestingly, there's one thing I already know about you for certain…

If you've read this book this far, I know you're interested in getting more prospects, customers, sales and profits from your business.

It's just a question of your willingness to take that small first step that's necessary for you to experience for yourself the benefits you'll receive from this truly one-of-a-kind program.

Look, I could go on and on trying to "sell you" (and maybe you expect me to), but that's not my style (you'll learn more about my approach to getting customers and clients in a much easier and enjoyable way when you signup, it's kind of like going fishing, but with a thousand poles in the water).

You don't have to decide now, just give it a try and then you be the judge.

Signup, get involved, take action on just a few things and convince yourself this is the best business decision you've ever made.

(continue reading on next page…)

Go ahead… Be good to yourself… Give it a try.

As always, my best to you –

Mark Hendricks

P.S. You really *can* increase your profits 50% or more in just a short period of time with these strategies properly implemented and managed correctly into your business.

P.P.S. Don't put this off – if you're like 96% of all business owners, you're not harvesting but a fraction of the profit potential that's hidden in your business. I'd like to help you too. Read this book again. These concepts can quickly get you more prospects, customers, sales and profits.

P.P.P.S. Not sure what to do? – don't decide now – just visit the website, look over everything (and give me a call if you really need to). Maybe you've got a question or two, or I didn't make something clear. Call me. The worst thing that could happen is you could learn a few new ways to increase your sales and profits – and that's not such a bad thing, is it?

Mark Hendricks, Hunteridge, Inc
P.O. Box 753 – 21450 Hendricks Lane, Trilby, FL 33593
Phone: 352-583-3697 Email: mark@smallbizsuccesscoach.com
Website: SmallBizSuccessCoach.com

www.ingramcontent.com/pod-product-compliance
Lightning Source LLC
Chambersburg PA
CBHW051255170526
45165CB00004B/1723